THE
PROBLEM BEHA
POCKETBOOK

By Angelena Boden
Drawings by Phil Hailstone

"Good management is not about getting your own way so much as getting the best out of your team. So, understanding what makes everyone tick - and recognising the signs when things start to go wrong - is vital. This little handbook is full of practical hints and early warning signs to help everyone on the team spot problems sooner rather than later."
Paul Field, Managing Director, UK Research Partnership Ltd

Published by:
Management Pocketbooks Ltd
14 East Street, Alresford, Hants SO24 9EE, U.K.
Tel: +44 (0)1962 735573   Fax: +44 (0)1962 733637
E-mail: pocketbks@aol.com
Web: www.pocketbook.co.uk

This edition published 1999

© Angelena Boden 1999

ISBN 1 870471 71 7

British Library Cataloguing-in-Publication Data – A catalogue record for this book
is available from the British Library.

Printed in U.K. by: Alresford Press Ltd, Prospect Road, Alresford, Hants

Author's Note

As a victim of problem behaviour, I write with some feeling about how damaging people's negative choice of words, tone of voice and actions can be at a personal, professional and corporate level.

Many of today's employees live in fear of going to work and have serious stress-related illnesses because their colleagues, managers and clients treat them badly.

We all have a responsibility to behave in a way that does not oppress or take away the rights or dignity of others.

We do not have to be victims. I hope that you will find some useful tips in this Pocketbook to identify and deal with some of the more common behavioural patterns found in the workplace.

Acknowledgements

Rev. Canon Keith Withington - for his patience, wisdom and understanding.
Dr. Martin Allen and Dr. Helen Armstrong - who never once believed it was all in my imagination.
To all my family and friends.
Finally, I dedicate this book to my daughters, Anousheh and Anisa.

CONTENTS

1 INTRODUCTION

WHAT IS BEHAVIOUR?

Behaviour is something we learn from childhood. We watch what our parents, relatives and other adults do and we copy. We have no idea whether it is right or wrong until someone tells us - and even then we are influenced by that person's own values. No wonder we get it wrong so many times!

Yet, despite this programming, we do have a **choice**.

It is easy to adopt a 'take me as you find me' attitude but this is not always appropriate. We have to alter our behaviour to suit the situation and the person - that is, if we wish to avoid trouble.

Whatever our choice, we are **responsible** for our behaviour and **accountable** for the consequences.

INTRODUCTION

CHOICE AFFECTS OTHERS

How we choose to behave affects other people. We may deliberately choose behaviours to annoy, anger and frustrate others or we may be driven by force of habit.

We don't always realise the impact our behaviour has on other people or we may choose to block it out.

EXAMPLES

+/–	Behaviour	Impact	Consequence
+	Delivering work on time	Smiles/thanks	Praise/more money
–	Abrasive tone	Sarcastic retort	Bad feeling in the office

(3)

NEGATIVE BEHAVIOUR AT WORK

Here are a few examples of negative behaviour:

- Regularly late
- Moody before first coffee
- Smoking when banned
- Over-critical
- Intimidating to get results
- Slamming doors and drawers, and shouting to release anger
- Silent and brooding for days

Ask yourself:

- Am I guilty of these or other behaviours? If so, note them down.
- Do they apply to people I know at work?
- Has anything been said or done?
- What is the impact on the team?

4

INTRODUCTION

WHY DO PEOPLE BEHAVE BADLY AT WORK?

This is a complex question with many theories and viewpoints.
Key reasons include:

- Subconscious replay of childhood behaviours
- Hidden agendas
- Acting out a role
- Feeling bad, which leads to acting badly
- Poor knowledge of good, helpful behaviours and their impact on people
- Bad behaviour is seen as a powerful means of control
- Strong feelings of fear, anger, inadequacy, inferiority and self-hatred
- Self-protection
- Attention-seeking

EFFECTS OF NEGATIVE BEHAVIOUR

Let's be honest, we can **all** act badly from time to time. It's all a matter of degree. When someone at work habitually bullies, dominates, flirts or acts dumb it can:

- Lower the morale of the workforce and possibly lead to illnesses
- Reduce productivity
- Impair quality
- Affect customer service
- Increase or create tension/friction
- Force good staff to leave
- Bring a small business to its knees

WHAT CAN MANAGEMENT DO ABOUT IT?

In general:
- Be **aware** of negative behaviours and **observe**
- Raise team morale (social gatherings, bonuses, staff awards)
- Keep lines of communication open (keep no secrets)
- Talk to all staff (meetings, individual chats, invite disclosures)
- Use formal procedures when necessary

Specifically:
- Ask the individuals concerned to discuss work/problems
- State that their behaviours have been noticed - give concrete examples
- Explain the effect it is having
- Ask what they propose to do about it
- Find out if they need help
- State clearly what will happen if things don't improve
- Carry it out

> Above all, **praise** their **good** points. This might be what they need to boost their self-esteem.

INTRODUCTION

STRESS & BEHAVIOUR

Increased stress and uncertainty can reinforce negative
behaviours. A quick-tempered person can become a
raging demon when severely stressed.

- Martyrs can be off work for weeks
- Minor conflicts can escalate into full-scale wars

Many organisations refuse to acknowledge
stress as being a problem for them and, yet,
people behaving badly can be a key sign
that something is seriously amiss.

THE BULLY

THE BULLY

BULLYING TYPES

'Only big, powerful men are bullies.' Wrong! Just about anyone can use bullying behaviour in the workplace, irrespective of status, age, qualifications, job title and responsibility.

The most usual example is that of a male manager who uses direct and open forms of bullying, eg: threats, sexual harassment and abusive language.

However, there are more subtle forms used by:

- Junior staff towards their managers
- Women towards men and each other
- Colleague to colleague at the same level

Bullies in all their guises are **made** and not **born**.

THE BULLY

ORIGINS OF THIS BEHAVIOUR

Like all forms of behaviour, bullying is **learned** in childhood from a very early age. It may be learned from adults or other children and is reinforced through TV, press, supposed role models and screen heroes.

Bullies have watched others use certain behaviours to frighten, manipulate and dominate people into giving them what they want.

Many bullies have been victims themselves of this type of behaviour and, at some point in their lives, 'the worm has turned'.

Whatever its origins, bullying is considered by the practitioner to be an acceptable way of treating people.

THE BULLY

WHY DO IT?

Fear and feelings of inadequacy, low self-esteem, and the need to be in control and wield power are the key reasons.

Bullying derives from an inability to express feelings and express ideas in a mature, adult way. Frustration builds up, feelings of anger and aggression burst out and old wounds from childhood come to the surface.

The bully's own weaknesses are **projected** onto the other person:

'You're an idiot' is more likely to mean 'I'm an idiot'.

Take strength from knowing this.

FORMS OF BULLYING

> **'Bully** - persecute or oppress by force or threats; pressure or coerce (a person) to do something'.

The Oxford Modern English Dictionary.

The TUC received about 5,000 calls from employees during one recent Christmas period, complaining of a wide range of bullying behaviours. The nature of the complaints ranged from not being allowed time off on Christmas Day through to constant criticism.

Bullying takes many forms, some of which are listed on the next page.

FORMS OF BULLYING

Verbal bullying: Mockery, humiliation, constant sarcasm, negative and unjustified criticism, put downs, swearing, teasing, personal comments, sexual innuendoes, racist and sexist references, threats, badgering - from mild to severe.

Examples of verbal abuse regarding:	
Status	'Don't forget who I am'
Knowledge	'I know ...?' (you don't)
Experience	'I can do it better' (than you ever will)
Ability to work the system	'One word to my mate in accounts and ...'

Physical bullying: Touching, grabbing, closed body language, getting too close, constant hovering, banging on tables, kicking furniture, glaring, blocking doorways, accidentally spilling drinks.

Emotional bullying: Constant anger, explosive temper, indifference, jealousy, vengefulness, ignoring, threatening, instilling fear, withdrawal, pulling rank, sulking, refusal.

THE BULLY

DEALING WITH IT
EMOTIONALLY

The first step is to recognise bullying, especially in its more subtle forms. Be sure that such behaviours are not one-off over-reactions, to which we're all entitled.

The second step is to **detach yourself emotionally**. Don't show how you feel. By showing emotion in your words, voice, body language, behaviour or actions you have given in and allowed yourself to become a victim.

The bully wants to see you suffer - that reinforces the power he or she has over you.

You are **not powerless**.

Don't ever allow yourself to think that you are at fault. You have done nothing to cause the bullying and don't deserve it. The bully is responsible.

THE BULLY

DEALING WITH IT

VERBALLY

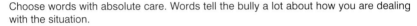

Choose words with absolute care. Words tell the bully a lot about how you are dealing with the situation.

Avoid words which:

Criticise	'You shouldn't ... you can't ... you've no right ...'
Demand	'You have to ... you'd better ...'
Threaten	'If you ... I'll ...'
Inflame	'Who the (*!*!*) do you think you are?'
Defer	'I'm sorry ... I didn't mean ...'
Mislead	'I'm not sure ... I can't remember'

Use words which are:

Positive and firm	'Yes, I did that. I believe it was right'
Assertive	'I intend to ...'
Direct	'Why are you ...?'
Courageous	'You can threaten as much as you like ...'

DEALING WITH IT
PHYSICALLY

- Make direct eye contact
- Use open body language - no fists, folded arms or nervous gestures
- Stand tall and firm - don't cower or flinch
- Walk away, go back to your desk, leave the room
- Keep your physical distance
- Don't copy or mirror the bully's behaviour (that's what bullies want you to do)

THE BULLY

DEALING WITH IT

THROUGH ACTIONS

- Start to collect evidence - log dates, times, locations, events
- Find someone senior to the bully, whom you can trust, and confide in that person
- Confront the bully, make a clear, unemotional statement of fact
- Stand firm against escalating threats (threats will increase as the bully fights to gain control)
- State your course of action but don't counter-threaten
- Carry out the action

At worst, look for another job.

Not doing anything makes you a party to the bullying.

THE MARTYR
& OVER-ZEALOUS

THE MARTYR

Playing the martyr at work is indulgent behaviour. Those that do so - usually women, particularly women in low-paid, low-grade jobs - are a lot cleverer than they realise.

Martyrs:

- Lack confidence in themselves, have low self-esteem and a poor understanding of their abilities and of their value

- Have poor communication skills, find it difficult to mix socially and are unable to express their needs assertively

- Find themselves apologising for things they haven't done

- Feel obliged to show gratitude to others

- Want people to feel sorry for them

Their behaviour leads other people to have negative feelings towards them. This reinforces the martyr's own sense of self-worth and the cycle is never broken.

THE MARTYR

WHY BE A MARTYR?

- To get sympathy, attention and praise from colleagues and managers
- From a desperate need to please, be liked and accepted
- For dependency
- To have control over others
- To have something to moan about
- From a subconscious reaction to feeling inadequate

Martyrdom is a way of punishing others by triggering their feelings of guilt, ie: make them feel bad too.

21

THE MARTYR

WHAT FORMS DOES MARTYRDOM TAKE?

The behaviour of the martyr is passive.

Verbal

- 'I suppose I'll have to do it.'
- 'I'm hopeless.'
- 'I'll never get the hang of this.'
- 'I tried my best.'
- 'I've got no choice.'

Non-verbal

- Sighing, tearful, drooped facial expression, low voice, stooped shoulders, fidgeting, hand ringing, covering the face, quivering lip, lowered gaze, refusing to join in/eat, range of physical complaints
- Looks wide-eyed and confused
- Plays the idiot

THE MARTYR & OVER-ZEALOUS

THE MARTYR

WHAT FORMS DOES MARTYRDOM TAKE?

Emotional
Mainly expressing self-pity and self-loathing rather than blaming others. Martyrs turn feelings in on themselves rather than project them onto others. They are still pretty cute at making you feel bad about it though.

Actions
- Indulging in a sulk lasting days, even weeks
- Suddenly leaving the room, a meeting, computer station
- Going quiet, refusing to add to the discussion
- Staying later at work, coming in earlier, offering to take on extra work but with a heavy sigh
- Agreeing with all criticism, taking on the role of scapegoat without question

Through his or her actions, the martyr says: 'Punish me, overload me, I'm bad'.
All very wearing.

THE MARTYR

WHAT YOU SHOULD DO

Once you have recognised it, realise that martyrdom is a form of manipulation, a subconscious game, even, designed to make others feel guilty.

- Don't feel guilt, pity or sympathy. The martyr knows what he/she is doing.
- State all requests, decisions and orders clearly and firmly. Provide an opportunity for the martyr to take issue there and then.
- Use open questions to challenge feelings, eg: 'What is the problem?' Don't take 'Nothing' for an answer as this gives the martyr permission to carry on.
- Firmly call for an end to the behaviour, eg: 'Stop sulking'.
- Don't let martyrs know that their moods are affecting others or the work. This will give them secret pleasure ('So it's working!' they will tell themselves).
- Do say 'It's affecting your future with us'.
- Don't question what you are doing. Martyrs easily undermine.
- Don't be taken in by sob-stories. The martyr has plenty of ammunition.

Get tough. Don't play their game.
Ignore them. They eventually stop.

24

THE OVER-ZEALOUS

'Look at me - how hard I am working.'

The motives of the over-zealous are similar to those of the martyr but the behaviours are the reverse. They include:

- Waiting until others leave at night, claiming to be hard at work: 'Can't possibly leave till ten'.
- Always appearing to enjoy being on overload.
- Piles of papers, books and files strewn on the desk. 'No time ... no time ...'
- Larger than life presence. Plenty of noise, back-slapping and loud conversations on the phone.
- Manic activity not always productive.
- Takes on more and more, wanting to show stamina, ability, loyalty, etc.

THE OVER-ZEALOUS

REASONS

The most logical explanation is ambition, wanting promotion. However, look below the surface and you will find:

- **Insecurity**   This person needs praise, positive responses that he or she didn't get as a child.

- **High anxiety level**   Fear of being overlooked, discounted, negated, dismissed.

The larger than life behaviours are to compensate for shyness and to make sure others take notice - another form of manipulative behaviour.

THE OVER-ZEALOUS
WHAT YOU SHOULD DO

- Set clear objectives with planned reviews.
- Carefully monitor working methods and relationships with others.
- Tackle the issue: 'You seem to be on edge. What is the problem?'
- Give praise for loyalty and commitment but be tough on quality issues.
- Change the work pattern. One project at a time with regular reviews.
- Give permission for the person to slow down.

THE MARTYR & OVER-ZEALOUS

EFFECTS ON THE WORKPLACE

The martyr and over-zealous are two sides of the same coin. Both have negative effects on the workplace.

The martyr:
- Adversely affects people's moods
- Lowers morale
- Wastes time by 'demanding' sympathy: 'What can we do to help?'
- Creates bad temper: 'For goodness sake - pull yourself together'

The over-zealous:
- Causes irritation
- Triggers strong reactions
- Generates hyperactivity amongst others, leading to poor attention to quality (everyone operates as if they are on stimulants just to keep up)
- Is feared: 'Better stay on if I want the promotion'

28

THE NARCISSIST

NARCISSISTIC BEHAVIOURS

Narcissus, you may recall, stopped to drink from a river, saw a beautiful reflection staring back at him and he promptly fell in love ... with himself!

(Echo had a lucky escape.)

Silly boy tried to entice his reflection from the water. Eventually he pined to death because he couldn't have the impossible. Sounds like anyone you know?

Narcissists are everywhere. We all have a bit of the narcissist in us otherwise we'd never achieve anything. However, it is usually a personality and behavioural trait exhibited by men (ouch!).

THE NARCISSIST

ORIGINS

A doting parent is usually behind narcissistic behaviour. Sons, especially first born, who are put on a pedestal, worshipped and protected, are in danger of developing these self-centred characteristics.

When narcissists reach the school of hard knocks, and it is pointed out that they are not as perfect as they had imagined, fragile egos are easily shattered. This often results in **narcissistic rage** (more about that later on).

THE NARCISSIST

BEHAVIOURAL SIGNS

- Quick to become angry over trivialities
- Refusal to listen to a viewpoint other than own
- Stubbornness to 'N'th' degree
- Total rigidity - can be very suspicious
- Contradictory and contrary
- Blames others for what goes wrong but is quick to claim praise
- Able to twist facts and sound convincing
- Almost impossible to reason with at times
- Will sulk and brood all day - maybe for weeks if things don't go his or her way
- Contemptuous of other people's ideas - uses ridicule as a put down
- Little ability to empathise or experience compassion
- Totally self-focused
- Uses others unashamedly for own ends
- Spends time preening in front of mirrors; always looking for approval

Remember, behind the superior façade is a frightened little person who can't really cope with life unless he or she is the centre of attention.

THE NARCISSIST

WHAT YOU SHOULD DO

Narcissists make excellent dictators. Give them a job, therefore, where the workforce will touch their forelocks on entering the office.

When they are given a bit of power they often do very well as this feeds their ego. If you've got debts to be collected, send your own Narcissus on the road - he'll terrify (or bore) people into paying up.

More seriously though ...

THE NARCISSIST

WHAT YOU SHOULD DO

HOW TO COMMUNICATE

- Keep it to a minimum. Language should be free of emotion and opinion. Stick to facts and keep repeating them until they sink in.
- Say 'no' as often as you need to.
- When they are wrong tell them so.
- Don't mirror their communication techniques - no scorn, ridicule, sarcasm, ranting or raving.
- Don't flatter or pay undue attention. Narcissists feed on compliments and like to play to an audience. Remain detached and nonchalant.
- Watch your body language - tell-tale signs of anger, aggression and frustration will be picked up. Maintain an inscrutable facial expression.

THE NARCISSIST

AVOIDING MANIPULATION & MIND GAMES

Narcissists love to play mind games. They twist facts, project blame and produce the most bizarre rationalisations, expressed with so much confidence!

- State your case and walk away.

- Pull down your mental guard (you are not going crazy - they want you to think that!).

- Don't allow yourself to be blackmailed or threatened. If they want to go to the CEO, then say 'That's fine'.

- Use all formal structures when necessary but be prepared for them to kick against the system.

- Imagine your narcissist in a giant nappy. It might not help the situation but it will stop you from gouging out the person's eyes!

THE NARCISSIST

NARCISSISM IN PRACTICE
EXAMPLE ONE

Example 1

You've arranged a staff lunch to celebrate Susie's forthcoming wedding. 'Narcissus' walks in late (on purpose), throws challenging looks at everyone, flicks a comb through his carefully coiffeured hair, straightens his tie and waits for everyone to stand up and say, 'We were really worried about you'.

Don't. Point to a chair, carry on with your conversation. Ignore this.

'Narcissus' will try to steal the show with a sarcastic comment. Ignore this. If the hint is not taken, then tell the person to grow up.

There is no polite or tactful way to deal with this behaviour. Narcissists are so pig headed, they only hear their own voice.

THE NARCISSIST

NARCISSISM IN PRACTICE
EXAMPLE TWO

Example 2

You are parking your faithful old car when 'Narcissus' arrives in an open-topped Porsche and parks in the spot marked 'Disabled'. Music is blaring out which the driver only turns down in order to answer the car phone.

You have two disabled visitors arriving shortly. The Porsche is in the way. What do you do?

Answer: report 'Narcissus' to security and pass no comment.

THE NARCISSIST

NARCISSISTIC RAGE

Narcissistic rage is a temper of extraordinary proportion, often involving banging doors, throwing cups, kicking the wastepaper bin, screaming at the staff and telling the MD to stuff the job (unless 'Narcissus' is the MD).

The force of anger is destructive, ongoing and out of control - just like the little child who couldn't have the last chocolate biscuit.

Roll your eyes and walk away.

Sometimes a bit of humiliation does the trick.

THE PASSIVE-AGGRESSIVE

THE PASSIVE-AGGRESSIVE

DESCRIPTION

This is a very effective form of behaviour that some people use to bring bosses and even companies to their knees.

How do they manage this?

Simply by doing **nothing** - effective but highly inefficient.

Even though passive-aggressive types have a weapon of extreme force they end up shooting themselves in the foot.

They are saboteurs, difficult to spot at first and can be very dangerous.

THE PASSIVE-AGGRESSIVE

ORIGINS OF THIS BEHAVIOUR

Next time you pop into your local supermarket watch how many toddlers are sitting down in the crisps and sweetie aisle, refusing to move another inch. Mum and dad beg and plead, bribe and threaten, but toddler stays put.

This is passive-aggressive behaviour in the making. The child is learning that by simply doing nothing at all it is possible to get mum and dad into such a state that they will do anything.

What should mum and dad do?

Start walking. Wave bye-bye and wait. The screams will get louder but toddler will get up, scream and reluctantly move.

THE PASSIVE-AGGRESSIVE

WHY & HOW

Why people behave like this
- It hides an anger which cannot be openly expressed
- The person has been brought up unable to say 'no'
- There is a subconscious desire to fail and be punished
- In-built laziness
- A strong wish to cause trouble and rebel, but not actively
- To take an indirect form of control

How they behave
- Put things off
- Arrive late
- Refuse to co-operate
- Lose things
- Conveniently forget
- Under-perform
- Pretend not to understand
- Miss appointments
- Keep silent in meetings - never show their hand
- Sit on the fence

THE PASSIVE-AGGRESSIVE

VERBAL CLUES

- Vague statements: 'Maybe', 'I'll have to think about it'.
- Set expressions that stop conversation: 'Good for you'; 'None of your business'.
- Circuitous language:
  'I didn't know about the meeting.'
  'You put it in your diary.'
  'What diary?'
  'Your day diary.'
  'I don't put meetings in that diary.'
  'Yes, you do. That's what it is for.'
  'Nobody told me that.'
  'Grrrrr ...'
- Grunts
- No communication at all

THE PASSIVE-AGGRESSIVE

NON-VERBAL CLUES

- No eye contact or very little. Can stare past insolently.
- Head down - pre-occupied with reading, doodling, fiddling.
- Fixed, rigid expression.
- Stiff body position.
- Almost no movement.

The big give away:

- Taunting little smiles.

THE PASSIVE-AGGRESSIVE

DEALING WITH IT

Passive-aggressives are very difficult to deal with. Underneath they are seething with resentment, full of frustration and have a big chip on their shoulders, especially when dealing with authority.

On the surface they seem quiet, unassuming types and can easily be mistaken for being non-threatening.

The more active and energetic you become with them the more stubborn they become.

The best advice is to **walk away**. This ends their **game**.

MORE PRACTICAL SOLUTIONS

Don't assume that when they say 'yes' they mean it.

- Give a clear explanation of what you want done and why
- Repeat it until you get a commitment
- Get an agreement in writing if necessary
- Give a deadline
- Check that progress is being made
- Stress the consequence of not performing
- Carry out 'punishments'

THE PASSIVE-AGGRESSIVE

GIVE THEM A DOSE OF THEIR OWN MEDICINE

- Pay them late
- Be late for an appointment with **them**
- Refuse to co-operate
- Pretend to misunderstand
- Conveniently 'forget' something they wanted

Then ask them how they **feel**.

If you are involved in an important project and have a passive-aggressive type working with you, but you are getting nowhere, **remove the person**.

THE PASSIVE-AGGRESSIVE

A FINAL WORD

Passive-aggressive types are both frustrating and frustrated.

They don't want to behave the way they do but they have a self-destruct button itching to be pressed.

The only people who can help these kamikaze types are the passive-aggressives themselves.

THE PERSISTENT
FAULT-FINDER

THE PERSISTENT FAULT-FINDER

WHATEVER YOU DO WILL BE WRONG

The fault-finder in the workplace is only distinguishable from the bully insomuch as he or she tends to attack the quality of the work rather than the person.

Fault-finding is practised throughout business by many people. They are fuelled by:

- A need to show they are 'on top of the job'
- A fear of showing their own weaknesses or lack of understanding
- A subconscious need to put people down in order to feel better about themselves
- Their drive for perfection

THE PERSISTENT FAULT-FINDER

VERBAL SIGNS

The language of persistent fault-finders ranges from mild comments to searing criticism.

- Open questions are used in an attempt to catch people off guard:

  'Have you noticed anything unusual in this drawing/proposal?'

- Tongue in cheek statements, while not being specific about a particular problem, trigger feelings of unease:

  'Either I was talking gobbledegook at the meeting or you were asleep?' (Flashing smile.)

- The fault-finder regularly uses expressions such as 'but', 'it's a shame' and 'what on earth?':

  'An excellent piece of work, Rodney. What a pity ...'

- Upward fault-finders choose less challenging language:

  'Silly you. Look how you've spelt ...!'

THE PERSISTENT FAULT-FINDER

NON-VERBAL LANGUAGE

Moods affect body language except when fault-finders set out to be manipulative.
Examples of their body language include:

Mild expressions   Head shaking, tutting, tapping teeth with pen, rolling eyes, half-smile, sighing, frowning

Moderate expressions   Closing eyes, grimacing, sudden movements, agitated hand gestures

Severe expressions   Pacing, throwing down pens, shaking fingers, dragging hands through hair

THE PERSISTENT FAULT-FINDER

BEHAVIOUR

The fault-finder's behaviour is often difficult to pin down as the other person is left with a bad feeling but can't find real evidence for it.

If the 'victim' asks for help and guidance the fault-finder may adopt the following tactics:

- Emotional and physical distancing - suddenly being unavailable
- Delegate mentoring to someone else
- Over-nurture
- Resort to bullying

THE PERSISTENT FAULT-FINDER

TYPICAL ACTIONS

- Moves goal-posts
- Denies or re-words anything previously said
- Pleads poor memory
- Sets people up for failure
- Never accepts blame - projects it instead
- Avoids dealing with issues
- Won't give straight answers on the spot
- Can't give praise but desperately needs it
- Makes sure that no matter how perfect the completed task, there is something wrong with it

THE PERSISTENT FAULT-FINDER

DEALING WITH THE FAULT-FINDER

People who are new to a company, recently promoted or hyper-sensitive to criticism need to ask themselves some questions when subjected to fault-finding:

- Is the criticism justified?
- How often has it happened over the last month?
- Could the fault-finder feel threatened by me?
- How well do I do my job?

If the fault-finder's comments are justified, accept them and treat the experience as part of your personal and professional development.

If not, and the criticism is becoming a regular occurrence, you need to take steps.

DEALING WITH THE FAULT-FINDER
EMOTIONALLY

Staying detached and not taking things personally is an essential first step.

- Keep your wits about you
- Talk to other people - see what they think of your work
- Don't engage in unnecessary conversation with the person
- Remind yourself daily of your achievements, not your failures - keep self-esteem high
- Stand up for yourself

THE PERSISTENT FAULT-FINDER

DEALING WITH THE FAULT-FINDER
VERBALLY

- Be straight. Use non-emotive language.
- Ask precise, closed questions.
- Paraphrase statements to check understanding. Show the fault-finder that you want to **improve**, not play a game.
- Request specific guidelines/instructions in writing if the matter is serious.
- Don't play the martyr by saying, 'I'm really sorry; I'm useless'.
- Take a direct approach, 'I want training and further information if I am to avoid this problem in the future'.

NON-VERBALLY

- Don't let your feelings show in your gestures or facial expressions!

THE PERSISTENT FAULT-FINDER

MESSAGE TO MANAGERS

Fault-finders home in on the most insecure of employees. Their behaviour undermines confidence and wears people down. This can affect a whole team. One day someone will turn round and say, **'Why don't you shut up?'** and blame management for not dealing with it.

Your task as a manager in dealing with persistent fault-finders is to:

- Listen, observe and root them out
- Tackle them head on
- Find out what **their** problem is
- Be direct in telling them to change their behaviour

THE PERSISTENT FAULT-FINDER

IF YOU ARE A FAULT-FINDER

Own up!

- Praise before criticism
- Don't look for faults
- Nurture, encourage and offer training
- Ask yourself why you are doing this

Fault-finding undermines and is destructive.

NOTES

Clams & Chatterers

CLAMS & CHATTERERS

WHO ARE THE CLAMS?

Clams are the most exasperating types of people to communicate with, especially when you need:

- Information to do a job
- Clear direction
- Approval
- To negotiate
- Help and advice
- Opinions
- A team to work together and co-operate

CLAMS & CHATTERERS

RECOGNISING THE CLAMS

- Tight-lipped, pinched faces. No eye contact provides the perfect defence for clams.
- They use silence to reject you. However reasonable your ideas, clams reject you personally.
- Stubborn refusal to talk other than to give one word answers when really pressed.
- Selective listening - they hear what they want to hear. This can be particularly difficult in meetings and at appraisals.
- No give-away clues in their body language.
- Emotionless.

WHAT TRIGGERS THE CLAM'S BEHAVIOUR?

- Something to hide (damaged the fax machine and won't own up or lies about it)
- Something about which the person is ashamed (an affair with the accounts manager)
- Can't face up to or accept an issue (redundancy)
- Protecting someone else
- Need to avoid a painful confrontation
- Not knowing how to communicate with you
- Afraid that whatever he or she says is wrong so it is safer to say nothing
- Lack of confidence

THE DAMAGE CLAMS CAN DO

It is difficult to imagine that people who say little can do much damage at all. However, clams can cause major upsets in a working environment by:

- Refusing to agree or disagree, thereby causing stalemate in decision-making

- Creating an uncomfortable atmosphere

- Not co-operating

- Sabotaging teamwork through non-involvement

- Not sharing expertise

- Indirectly increasing the stress levels of colleagues because of the frustration they experience

DEALING WITH CLAMS

Unless you have the patience of Job your gut reaction will be to lose your temper and shake such people until they rattle. Above all, bite your lip until it bleeds, if you have to, and stay cool.

- Don't insult and put them down.
- Ask **open** questions. Be prepared for a long wait for the reply. Repeat the question.
- Stay polite.
- Enlist their help: 'I value your opinion'.
- Acknowledge their strengths: 'You have a lot of expertise to bring to this project'.
- Don't waffle. Plan what you want to say and stick to it.
- Avoid being threatening.

CLAMS & CHATTERERS

DEALING WITH CLAMS

- Keep your voice even but low. Clams retreat further into their shell if you shout or sound agitated.

- Make eye-contact and smile. Keep gestures to a minimum.

- Keep physical distance. Clams feel threatened easily.

- Use active listening and evaluation gestures (eg: nodding, chin stroking and head to one side) and position yourself on the same level.

- Avoid whispering or throwing sideways glances towards the clam. This will increase their suspicions.

DEALING WITH CLAMS

Clams have an automatic reject mechanism - their perception of the world is two dimensional, black and white, If they don't like one aspect of you or your work they will reject you without taking into account the good points. In fact, they won't see the good points.

Clams are arrogant enough to believe that their opinion of people is right and that everyone should share it. They are truly amazed to learn that this is not the case.

You **can't** get them to change their minds but you **can** let them see that their behaviour, which is fed by this rigid attitude, does not affect you and that they are not superior to you - as they would like to believe.

DEALING WITH CLAMS

Clams use their silence as a weapon to manipulate and for self-protection. They know people will lose their patience and will resort to abuse and shouting, therefore their silence is justified.

Throw them off balance by:

- Not reacting
- Staying objective - ignoring their game
- Giving them quality attention - making them feel as if they belong and they are valued
- Smiling in a friendly way
- Including them even when they reject you

THE CONSTANT CHATTERERS

At the other end of the spectrum are the people who can't shut up. They come into work chatting and take every opportunity (during a break, on the phone, at the photocopier, in the lift) to chat ... chat ... chat.

What do they talk about? Usually nothing to do with work:

- Everything and nothing
- Everyone
- How terrible everything is
- Their hopes and fears
- Relationships, children, life

WHAT TRIGGERS THE CHATTERER'S BEHAVIOUR?

In a word **nerves**.

Unlike the clams, the chatterers can't bear silence. It unnerves them. They have to fill in the gaps in conversation, think aloud or make some noise. They need to be **noticed**, listened to and praised.

Chatterers need to be reassured that their work is fine, that relationships are harmonious and that they haven't upset anyone.

They have an automatic connection mechanism - an open mouth!

THE DAMAGE CHATTERERS CAN DO

- Irritate colleagues - 'Why can't he/she shut up?'
- Reduce work performance
- Reduce focus and concentration
- Reduce productivity
- Cause disorganisation
- Cause timescales to slip
- Generate frustration and anger

In effect, chatterers have a similar impact to that of clams.

DEALING WITH CHATTERERS

Chatterers in the work environment are draining. They feel they are endearing themselves to people but, in fact, the reverse is happening. Colleagues grit their teeth and suppress the desire to strangle them.

- Use closed questions - invite 'yes/no' answers.
- Stick to the topic - plan what you are going to say.
- State firmly what you require. Give deadlines.
- Give praise - this often takes the wind out of their sails.
- If the problem is serious put them in with a clam (in a separate office).

DEALING WITH CHATTERERS

- Stop giving encouraging signals for them to continue - reduce eye contact.
- Walk away.
- Send memos by e-mail. Ask for replies by same route.
- Keep them busy.
- Increase levels of responsibility.
- Stop what you are doing and walk slowly to their desk. This is the signal for them to stop talking.
- Regularly monitor their progress.
- Move them around to other areas of work if it is practical. If they have to focus on learning something new it can concentrate the mind. Chatterers are often bored and don't know what to do about it.

Basic rule
Don't give them too much encouragement otherwise they will go on and on and on (longer than a famous brand of battery).

MOANERS
COMPLAINERS & WHINGERS

MOANERS, COMPLAINERS & WHINGERS

RECOGNISING THEM

The world is full of them! The weather, the traffic, the economy, the office coffee, the workload, 'her in finance' - if they haven't got something to moan about they will find it.

Complainers aren't particularly difficult to deal with. It's their negative approach to everything that drags people down.

Unlike the fault-finder, who uses a surgical approach to cutting people down to size, or the martyr, who uses his or her behaviour to manipulate and get sympathy, the moaners just moan on .. and on ...

It's not just a habit - more of a disease.

MOANERS, COMPLAINERS & WHINGERS

MOANERS

Moaners can't help themselves. Often they don't even know they are doing it. You hear them everywhere: 'Why have I/do I/should I?'.

'Why' is a very moany word. We learn it when we are about three years old: 'But why..y..y daddy?'.

'Why' is used as a rhetorical question - so don't answer!

Facial expressions are very telling: narrowed eyes, puckered mouth, accompanying hand gestures - not a pretty sight.

COPING WITH MOANERS

Moaners can really get on your nerves! So tell them this in a calm, cool tone of voice. They will most likely apologise and then find someone to moan to about you being in a mood.

- Don't get agitated - this will make them worse
- Don't sympathise - this will encourage
- Stay neutral
- If other staff are affected, take the moaner to one side and ask direct questions using good eye contact:

    'People are fed up with your moaning. What is the problem?'
    'Have you finished the project?'
    'What time did you get into work?'
    'Did you telephone Accounts as I asked?'

This should make them focus.

ORIGINS OF MOANER'S BEHAVIOUR

Lack of attention as a child is the usual cause of a moaner's behaviour. No one listened properly or the child was perhaps dismissed frequently with a casual 'Yes, dear, very nice, now run along'.

Moaning can be a form of self-hypnosis - a well-rehearsed speech launched into on auto pilot. The mere mention of a name or a particular subject can launch the moaner off.

Probably, he or she has been told to shut up so many times that it has lost its effect.

Generally, moaners are people who feel empty, restless and bored - never satisfied, never content. The good things in life must have a catch.

WHAT FORM DOES MOANING TAKE?

- Blame, accusations
- Protestations of innocence
- Suggestions of injustice
- Defeatism: 'Can't be done'
- Pessimism: 'What do you expect?'
- Defensiveness: 'Can't have been me'
- Pushing off responsibility onto someone else
- Pure negative energy

COMPLAINERS

Complaining is more direct than moaning and should be easier to deal with.

- **Genuine complainers** can be very helpful. They want change and improvements and are usually prepared to make suggestions.
- **Aggressive complainers** hide behind their strong feelings and attack before they are attacked.
- **Passive complainers** allow a bad situation to get out of hand before they speak out.
- **Constructive complainers** are always looking for fault even when it is not necessary.

MOANERS, COMPLAINERS & WHINGERS

HOW TO MANAGE COMPLAINERS

- Listen to what they are saying
- Give feedback and paraphrase to ensure understanding
- Sift through the dross to get to the facts
- Throw the ball into their court: 'What do you suggest?'
  'What action do you want?'
- Ask them to go away and work on a concrete solution
- Get them to look at the problem from **all** angles -
  not just theirs
- Agree a **realistic** solution

Important
- Show you are receptive to their problems
- Stay detached and calm even when you are
  being blamed
- Empower or encourage them to take
  responsibility for their own problems

MOANERS, COMPLAINERS & WHINGERS

WHINGERS

Whingers are more annoying than moaners because of their whiny, high-pitched tone of voice. It is very child-like behaviour, often used to get attention or to present an 'I am helpless' position. They can be very trying because of their refusal to try out new things.

What to do?

- Don't be too hard on them or they will cry!
- Give them clear and firm instructions.
- Ignore the sulking, pained expressions and muttering.

Sometimes, making them angry helps break the cycle of negative thinking.

NOTES

THE POWER MAD,
CONTROL FREAK
& DICTATOR

THE POWER MAD, CONTROL FREAK & DICTATOR

PROFILE

The behaviours of these characters, while varying in degree and manner, are very similar and share the same end goal: ensuring the safety of the individuals concerned at the risk of others around them.

These people are not only found at the head of major corporations! Office managers, IT 'fix-its' and even the person in charge of the tea trolley may exhibit claims of territory.

At the extreme end of the spectrum you might come across the occasional 'sociopath' - not the axe-wielding monster but the person with very little conscience or feelings for others. Their behaviour is truly obnoxious.

There is little you can do to influence them.

THE POWER MAD, CONTROL FREAK & DICTATOR

WHAT TRIGGERS THEIR BEHAVIOURS?

The behavioural triggers of the power mad, control freak and dictator represent, for many, a painful journey: loss of control, inability to cope, betrayal and mistakes in a previous life may have triggered a great **fear** of losing control.

Controllers over-compensate, roar loudly to frighten off potential threats and are fuelled with the need to build an empire to protect them.

Observe them carefully and you will notice paranoid behaviours.

THE POWER MAD, CONTROL FREAK & DICTATOR

RECOGNISING THEIR BEHAVIOURS

- Need to control at all levels - from how the company accounts are prepared to how the tea is made
- Great reluctance to share
- Secretiveness
- Not providing access (keys, passwords, operational instructions, etc) even when it is demanded
- Use of verbal force (orders/abuse) to ward off questioning
- Use of threats to maintain position ('All those who enter here ...')
- Very little involvement, co-operation, negotiation or rational discussion
- Undermining others to build territory (today the photocopier, tomorrow the boardroom)
- Very little socialisation - rarely seen at office parties except to talk to the right people
- Totally focused on self

THE POWER MAD, CONTROL FREAK & DICTATOR

CONSTANT DRIVE TO STAY IN CONTROL

Look out for people who:

- Work extremely long hours and are in regular contact with powerful people
- Surround themselves with a few loyal 'yes' people
- Seem to be working to a different agenda compared with everyone else
- Use ruthless tactics to restructure, downsize, merge, acquire, develop and then **dump**
- Don't listen, talk against the flow and use bully-like tactics
- Are extreme passive-aggressives - this behaviour is very controlling

THE POWER MAD, CONTROL FREAK & DICTATOR

EFFECTS ON THE WORKPLACE

- An atmosphere of distrust and fear can build up
- People spend time trying to outwit the 'powerful one' and not getting on with their work
- Conspiracies are organised
- Morale drops - people disaffected
- Anxieties about job security increase - gradual loss of an experienced workforce
- Serious divisions between managers and workforce intensify

THE POWER MAD, CONTROL FREAK & DICTATOR

HOW TO COPE

The power-intoxicated have a big problem with **trust**.

While bullies see individuals as 'fair game' to wind up and frighten for no real personal gain, controllers see people as obstacles to personal progress and success. They are suspicious of talk and reasonable suggestions, and prefer to dominate, dictate and, if necessary, intimidate. Any hint of compromise would cause them to lose their balance.

If you are working for or with them:

- Say '**no**', citing reasons. Refuse to be intimidated. This will be a new experience for these people who are used to getting their own way.
- Show them you are not out to block their way.
- Be **open** and polite but keep your distance.
- Avoid criticism and give support where necessary. Compliment (they won't believe you but it's worth trying).
- Don't challenge - get on with your own work.
- Go to a higher authority if it gets too much.
- Look after yourself. Working with these people is mentally and emotionally draining.

MANAGING CONTROL FREAKS

Be cautious at the interview stage. Listen to their ambitions and how they would like to turn the company around. Is there a power-mad manager waiting to burst out?

- Draw very precise boundaries. Make it clear that their responsibility stops **here**.
- **Empower** with caution. Keep a tight rein on activities.
- Be precise about instructions - put them in writing so that they cannot be misinterpreted. If necessary, have witnesses.
- Use performance reviews regularly to clarify progress.
- Listen to other colleagues - pick up on the signs early.
- If the behaviour becomes a real problem, restructure.

PERSECUTOR, VICTIM
& RESCUER

SUBCONSCIOUS BEHAVIOUR PATTERNS

Finally, a more complex topic - the subconscious behaviour patterns within interpersonal relationships.

It is not only in the workplace that the roles of top-dog (persecutor) and under-dog (victim) are played out. At home, in social settings and in everyday interactions, these dramatic performances can be observed too.

Both role players manipulate other people and both strive to control.

PERSECUTOR

In adopting this role the person fixes tight boundaries on another's behaviour and enforces the rules without mercy.

Persecutors set out to make their victims feel bad/guilty, forced to justify their actions and provoked into responding in a certain way.

Persecutors always believe they are right, always play the righteous, are very authoritarian and use bully tactics (eg: threats).

If you feel you are being persecuted **don't play the victim!** Deal with persecutors as you would bullies.

This stops the game.

VICTIM

This role is also played to manipulate. Even though victims claim to be in a weaker position, they are, in fact, stronger than persecutors. Their strength lies in cunning, defensiveness, whining and being over-apologetic.

'I really did try.' 'I can't help being useless.'

Victims often seek out a persecutor to reinforce their position. Many people have learned from childhood to play victim in order to get what they want.

To be able to say, 'This is what they have done to me' is to be a winner in their eyes. Victims want to come out blameless and helpless.

The roles of persecutor and victim are interchangeable. Victims often persecute others.

Extreme victim behaviours can result in paranoia.

PERSECUTOR, VICTIM & RESCUER

RESCUER

Rescuers try to extract victims from persecutors and then end up getting kicked themselves:

'I was only trying to help,' they cry.

If you find yourself in the role of rescuer ask yourself what you are trying to achieve. Don't get caught up in psychological dramas, the origins of which are complicated and rooted in childhood experiences. Persistent game-playing of this nature requires professional help.

97

NOTES

MANAGING PROBLEM BEHAVIOUR

PROTECT YOUR STOMACH

In this pocketbook we have explored a number of techniques to adopt when faced with the range of difficult behaviours. However, the best way to prepare yourself is by getting out your suit of armour, checking it for holes, polishing it up and fastening it firmly around your stomach.

Why stomach? Because this is where bad feelings and reactions are stored. Don't you run to the loo when you've had an argument or you have to face a difficult boss?

BELIEVE IN YOURSELF

Hearing abuse or being rejected or bullied can lead to sensitive people thinking that they deserve it. Then they start believing it and eventually start acting as though they do.

Being told 'You're lazy' enough times will make you act lazy.

Think positively about yourself and about the situation. Matters can be resolved if you believe they can.

Think positively about the difficult person - hard to do but it helps to prevent a build up of your own antagonism.

MANAGING PROBLEM BEHAVIOUR

DESENSITISE & REPROGRAMME YOURSELF

- Tune out abusive remarks. They are only words, even though they hurt.

- Stay calm and don't give your 'opponents' the satisfaction of seeing you react in front of them (deal with your feelings later).

- Change your automatic negative emotional response to a positive one (with humour, if you can).

Example 1

	'You must be really thick if you can't make sense of that.'
Trigger	
Old response	'How dare you ...'
New response	Laughter.

BELOW-THE-BELT VERBAL ABUSE

Some people can resort to real below-the-belt stuff. They attack your intelligence, sanity, race, gender, appearance and understanding. Expose your Achilles' heel and they'll stick their verbal dagger in it.

Negative trigger words threaten self-esteem and personal image, even if our logical brain tells us otherwise.

We make associations between words and feelings that go back to childhood. As a child, did you get called lazy, no good and a waste of space? If so, that's why you react today when someone 'pulls your strings'.

KNOW YOUR TRIGGERS

We all have our triggers - words, expressions, a look in the eye - which press that button marked **blast off**.

If you want to see sparks coming from my eyes, just call me **stupid**.

Your key task:

Ask yourself: 'What hurts me most? Why? How do I react?'

Get to know your triggers and work on neutralising them.

DISASSOCIATE YOURSELF

- Disconnect the flow of negative energy from your thoughts, emotions and actions, and disconnect yourself from the situation.

- Begin a closing down process.

- Neutralise your feelings.

- Take a clinical approach.

- Deal with the situation in the here and now rather than as a painful reminder of a past event.

- Imagine the other person naked, hanging upside down from a tree, or as a tiny, harmless ant if it helps you to change your perception of their psychological power.

- Above all, make use of amused detachment. There's nothing like humour to turn difficult behaviour into something manageable.

About the Author

Angelena Boden BA, M.Soc.Sc., PGCE
Angelena is a freelance trainer in customer service, language
and culture, and people behaviour. This is her third Pocketbook
and one she feels is very much needed in business today.

Angelena writes from first-hand experience and is well aware
of the damage that difficult behaviour (she prefers to separate
people from their behaviour) can do to self-esteem,
confidence and morale.

She runs a range of one day seminar programmes - how to
deal with difficult people; coping in a crisis; advanced
communication for difficult situations - and a range
of tailor-made courses for industry.

Contact
Angelena's contact details are:
63 Bunbury Road, Northfield,
Birmingham B31 2DS
E-mail: one@angelenaboden.free-online.co.uk

ORDER FORM

Your details

Name _____

Position _____

Company _____

Address _____

_____

_____

Telephone _____

Facsimile _____

E-mail _____

VAT No. (EC companies) _____

Your Order Ref _____

Please send me:

		No. copies
The Problem Behaviour	Pocketbook	
The _____	Pocketbook	
The _____	Pocketbook	
The _____	Pocketbook	
The _____	Pocketbook	

Order by Post

MANAGEMENT POCKETBOOKS LTD
14 EAST STREET ALRESFORD HAMPSHIRE SO24 9EE UK

Order by Phone, Fax or Internet

Telephone: +44 (0)1962 735573
Facsimile: +44 (0)1962 733637
E-mail: pocketbks@aol.com
Web: www.pocketbook.co.uk

Customers in USA should contact:
Stylus Publishing, LLC, 22883 Quicksilver Drive,
Sterling, VA 20166-2012
Telephone: 703 661 1581 or 800 232 0223
Facsimile: 703 661 1501 E-mail: styluspub@aol.com

THE MANAGEMENT POCKETBOOK SERIES